کینیڈا میں اُردو کا سلسلہ وار نصاب

بچّوں کے لیے اُردو کی دوسری کتاب

آئیں اُردو لِکھیں

(دُوسرا حصّہ)

مدیرِ اعلیٰ

ڈاکٹر ساجدہ علوی

معاونین

فرحت احمد ۔ فاروق حسن ۔ اشفاق حسین

مجلسِ مصنّفین

حمیرہ انصاری ۔ فردوس بیگ ۔ رشیدہ مرزا ۔ حامدہ سیفی ۔ زاہدہ مرتضیٰ

تزئین کار : روپرٹ بو ٹنبرگ

فہرستِ مضامین

سہیلی بُوجھ پہیلی

میں   اپنے   سب   درختوں   کو   گِنوں   گی

میں   اپنے   سب   درختوں   کو   گِنوں   گی

میں   اپنے   سب   درختوں   کو   گِنوں   گی

میں   اپنے   سب   درختوں   کو   گِنوں   گی

ارم کو ایک نئ دوست مل گئ

ارم کو ایک نئ دوست مل گئ

ارم کو ایک نئ دوست مل گئ

ارم کو ایک نئ دوست مل گئ

_____

_____

_____

_____

_____

پارک

بائیسکل

سنگترہ

قَلعہ

پَری

وَرزِش

بھائی بھلکڑ

غائب	تو	جوتا	ہے	ٹوپی

| غائب | جوتا | تو | ہے | ٹوپی |

| غائب | جوتا | تو | ہے | ٹوپی |

| غائب | جوتا | تو | ہے | ٹوپی |

_____

_____

_____

_____

_____

جوتا   ہے   تو   موزا   غائب

جوتا   ہے   تو   موزا   غائب

جوتا   ہے   تو   موزا   غائب

جُوتا   ہے   تو   موزا   غائب

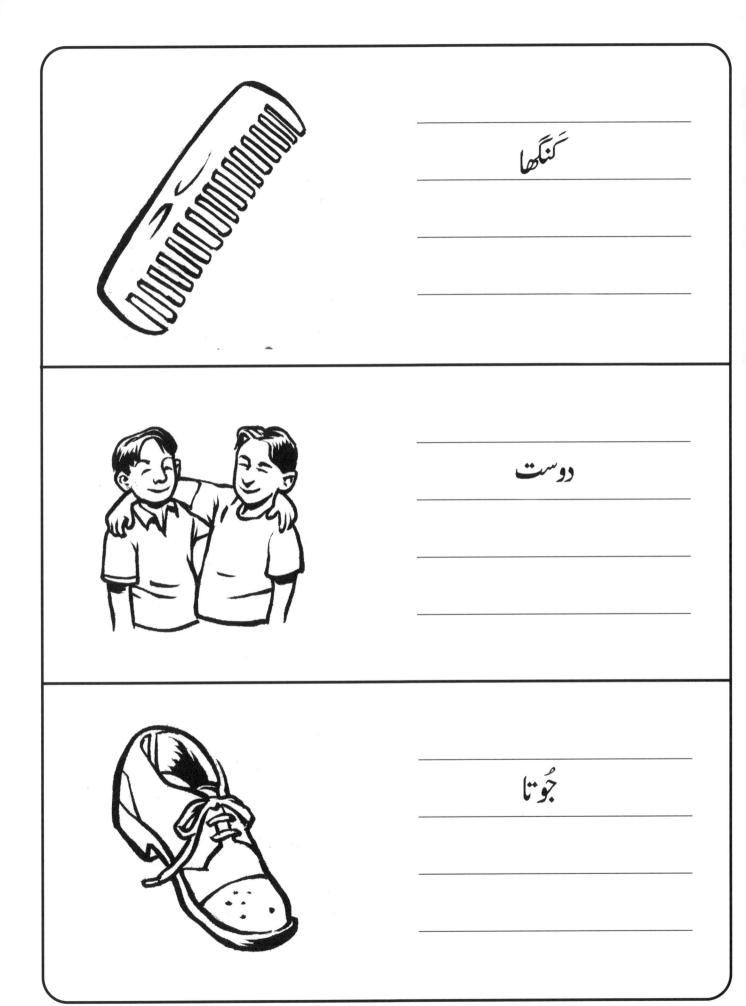

کَنگھا

دوست

جُوتا

11

بَستہ

چَمچہ

راستہ

نیلوفر کے گھر میں ایک تالاب تھا

نیلوفر کے گھر میں ایک تالاب تھا

نیلوفر کے گھر میں ایک تالاب تھا

نیلوفر کے گھر میں ایک تالاب تھا

جنگل   کے   جانور   بہت   خوش   تھے

جنگل   کے   جانور   بہت   خوش   تھے

جنگل   کے   جانور   بہت   خوش   تھے

جنگل   کے   جانور   بہت   خوش   تھے

عورت

حَوِیلی

جَھونپڑی

بِستر

مگرمچھ

ہِرن

ہمدردی

تنہا   کی   پہ   شجر   کسی   پہ   ٹہنی

تنہا   رگی   شجر   کسی   پہ   ٹہنی

تنہا   کی   شجر   کسی   پہ   ٹہنی

تنہا   کی   شجر   کسی   پہ   ٹہنی

بیٹھا	اُداس	کوئی	تھا	بُلبُل
بیٹھا	اُداس	کوئی	تھا	بُلبُل
بیٹھا	اُداس	کوئی	تھا	بُلبُل
بیٹھا	اُداس	کوئی	تھا	بُلبُل

_____

_____

_____

_____

_____

شَجَر

بُلبُل

رات

جُگنو

آشیاں

خالد اور نومی نے مِل کر روباٹ بنایا

خالد اور نومی نے مِل کر روباٹ بنایا

خالد اور نومی نے مِل کر روباٹ بنایا

خالد اور نومی نے مِل کر روباٹ بنایا

اُن کے روباٹ کا نام سبز باغ تھا

اُن کے روباٹ کا نام سبز باغ تھا

اُن کے روباٹ کا نام سبز باغ تھا

اُن کے روباٹ کا نام سبز باغ تھا

كِتابیں

_____

_____

_____

تصویریں

_____

_____

_____

رَوبَاٹ

_____

_____

_____

سنگھار میز

کپڑوں کی دراز

آیا جھڑ آیا پَت جھڑ پَت

آیا جھڑ پَت آیا جھڑ پَت

آیا جھڑ پَت آیا جھڑ پَت

آیا جھڑ پَت آیا جھڑ پَت

لایا	پتّے	برنگے	رنگ
لایا	پتّے	برنگے	رنگ
لایا	پتّے	برنگے	رنگ
لایا	پتّے	برنگے	رنگ

پتّے

خزاں

ہَوا

سورج چاند اور زمین آپس میں اچھے دوست تھے

سورج چاند اور زمین آپس میں اچھے دوست تھے

سورج چاند اور زمین آپس میں اچھے دوست تھے

سورج چاند اور زمین آپس میں اچھے دوست تھے

زمین کس وجہ سے اداس ہو گئی تھی ؟

زمین کس وجہ سے اداس ہو گئی تھی ؟

زمین کس وجہ سے اداس ہو گئی تھی ؟

زمین کس وجہ سے اداس ہو گئی تھی ؟

_____

_____

_____

_____

_____

سُورج

دھرتی

چاند

آسمان

یہ دو دن میں کیا ماجرا ہوگیا

یہ دو دن میں کیا ماجرا ہوگیا

یہ دو دن میں کیا ماجرا ہوگیا

یہ دو دن میں کیا ماجرا ہوگیا

کہ   جنگل   کا   جنگل   ہرا   ہو   گیا

کہ   جنگل   کا   جنگل   ہرا   ہو   گیا

کہ   جنگل   کا   جنگل   ہرا   ہو   گیا

کہ   جنگل   کا   جنگل   ہرا   ہو   گیا

برسات

پیڑ

پھل

جَڑی بُوٹی

کِسان

گھٹا

بیل

پُھول

صفی میاں کا فارم

پیٹ بھرے گا جب گائے کا

پیٹ بھرے گا جب گائے کا

پیٹ بھرے گا جب گائے کا

پیٹ بھرے گا جب گائے کا

دودھ   مِلے   گا   تب   گائے   کا

دودھ   مِلے   گا   تب   گائے   کا

دودھ   مِلے   گا   تب   گائے   کا

دودھ   مِلے   گا   تب   گائے   کا

شہر

گائے

فارم

پَنِیر

مَکَّھن

دُودھ

ایک   دیہاتی   بندر   کا   بچہ   بیچ   رہا   تھا

ایک   دیہاتی   بندر   کا   بچہ   بیچ   رہا   تھا

ایک   دیہاتی   بندر   کا   بچہ   بیچ   رہا   تھا

ایک   دیہاتی   بندر   کا   بچہ   بیچ   رہا   تھا

_____

_____

_____

_____

احمد کو بندر کا بچہ پسند آیا

احمد کو بندر کا بچہ پسند آیا

احمد کو بندر کا بچہ پسند آیا

احمد کو بندر کا بچہ پسند آیا

پہاڑی

گھر

بَطَّخ

بَندر

وادی

روٹی

گملا

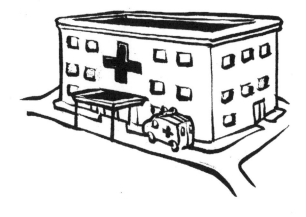

ہَسپتال

رحیم اور کریم کا کہیں پتہ نہ تھا

رحیم اور کریم کا کہیں پتہ نہ تھا

رحیم اور کریم کا کہیں پتہ نہ تھا

رحیم اور کریم کا کہیں پتہ نہ تھا

گھر والے خوشی سے ایک دوسرے سے لپٹ گئے

گھر والے خوشی سے ایک دوسرے سے لپٹ گئے

گھر والے خوشی سے ایک دوسرے سے لپٹ گئے

گھر والے خوشی سے ایک دوسرے سے لپٹ گئے

فہرست

کِھلونے

الارم

دُوکان

چوکیدار

گُڑیا گھر

شاپنگ پلازا

بَتّی

مریم کیمپنگ کے لیے جنگل جاتی تھی

مریم کیمپنگ کے لیے جنگل جاتی تھی

مریم کیمپنگ کے لیے جنگل جاتی تھی

مریم کیمپنگ کے لیے جنگل جاتی تھی

رضاکار مل کر پگڈنڈی بنا رہے تھے

رضاکار مل کر پگڈنڈی بنا رہے تھے

رضاکار مل کر پگڈنڈی بنا رہے تھے

رضاکار مل کر پگڈنڈی بنا رہے تھے

ملکہ

ندی

لکڑی

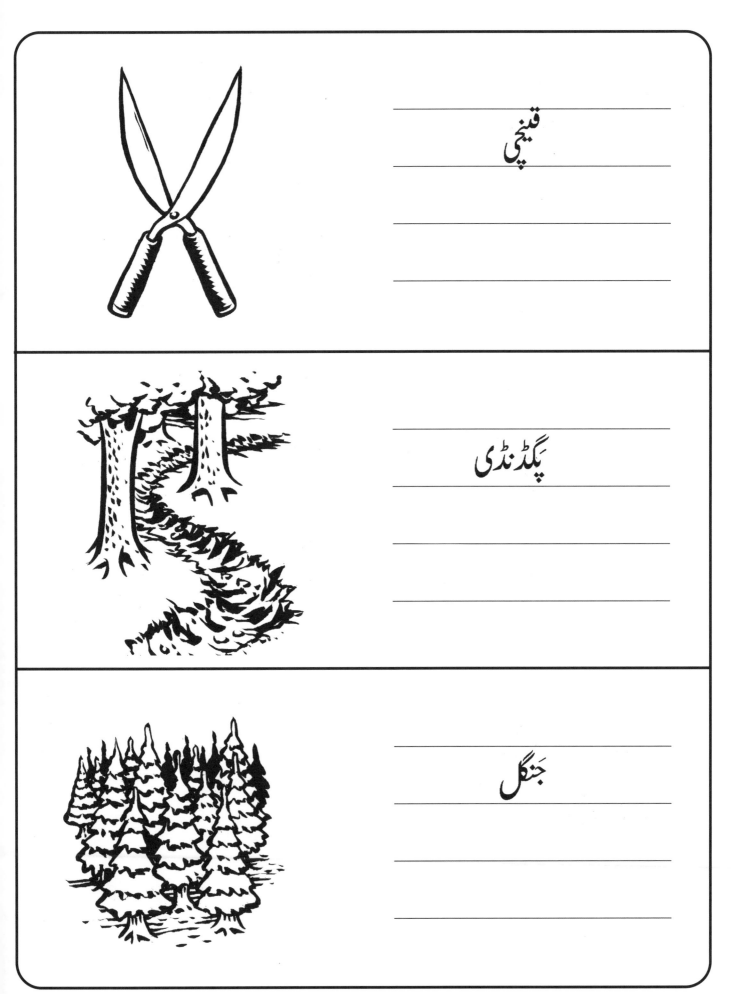

قینچی

پگڈنڈی

جَنگل

گرمی کی چھٹیاں

ہلکے   ہلکے   پہلے   کودیں   سیدھے   پاؤں   سے

سے   سے   پاؤں   سیدھے   کودیں   پہلے   ہلکے   ہلکے

ہلکے   ہلکے   پہلے   کودیں   سیدھے   پاؤں   سے

ہلکے   ہلکے   پہلے   کودیں   سیدھے   پاؤں   سے

دھیرے دھیرے آگے جائیں اُلٹے پاؤں سے

دھیرے دھیرے آگے جائیں اُلٹے پاؤں سے

دھیرے دھیرے آگے جائیں اُلٹے پاؤں سے

دھیرے دھیرے آگے جائیں اُلٹے پاؤں سے

گھوڑا

ٹوٹم پول

اصلی باشندے

بھینسا

دھول

جھالر

ساحل پر سفید ریت دُھوپ میں چمک رہی تھی

ساحل پر سفید ریت دُھوپ میں چمک رہی تھی

ساحل پر سفید ریت دُھوپ میں چمک رہی تھی

ساحل پر سفید ریت دُھوپ میں چمک رہی تھی

سب نے ایک درخت کی چھاؤں میں ڈیرہ لگا لیا

سب نے ایک درخت کی چھاؤں میں ڈیرہ لگا لیا

سب نے ایک درخت کی چھاؤں میں ڈیرہ لگا لیا

سب نے ایک درخت کی چھاؤں میں ڈیرہ لگا لیا

جُھنڈ

کھائی

ڈھانچہ

اِگوانا

ساحل

گردن   ہو   زرّافے   جیسی   بلّی   جیسی   مُونچھ

گردن   ہو   زرّافے   جیسی   بلّی   جیسی   مُونچھ

گردن   ہو   زرّافے   جیسی   بلّی   جیسی   مُونچھ

گردن   ہو   زرّافے   جیسی   بلّی   جیسی   مُونچھ

جو بھی اُس کو دیکھے سمجھے یہ ہے اصلی مُونچھ

جو بھی اُس کو دیکھے سمجھے یہ ہے اصلی مُونچھ

جو بھی اُس کو دیکھے سمجھے یہ ہے اصلی مُونچھ

جو بھی اُس کو دیکھے سمجھے یہ ہے اصلی مُونچھ

طَوطا

زرّافہ

مُوٗنچھیں

ٹوپی

بَرف کا آدمی

جُوتے

مَفلَر

برف

عامر اور مائیکل سرکس گئے

عامر تم یہاں کھڑے کیا کر رہے ہو ؟

عامر تم یہاں کھڑے کھڑے لگیا اگر رہے ہو ؟

عامر تم یہاں کھڑے کیا کر رہے ہو ؟

عامر تم یہاں کھڑے کیا کر رہے ہو ؟

_____

_____

_____

_____

_____

چلو سرکس شروع ہونے والا ہے

چلو سرکس شروع ہونے والا ہے

چلو سرکس شروع ہونے والا ہے

چلو سرکس شروع ہونے والا ہے

جنگلا

پنجرہ

حلقہ

خَیمہ

سِیٹی

قُلابازی

مَداری

مَسخَرہ

ساره نے کہا میں ایک جَل پَری ہوں

ساؤہ نے کہا میں ایک جَل پَری ہوں

ساؤہ نے کہا میں ایک جَل پَری ہوں

ساره نے کہا میں ایک جَل پَری ہوں

سمندر کی تہہ میں میرا محل ہے

سمندر کی تہہ میں میرا محل ہے

سمندر کی تہہ میں میرا محل ہے

سمندر کی تہہ میں میرا محل ہے

جل پری

سمُندر

مَحَل

سیپ

موتیوں کا ہار

بلّی کا انوکھا بچّہ

جمیلہ   پارک   میں   جھُولا   جھُول   رہی   تھی

جمیلہ   پارک   میں   جھُولا   جھُول   رہی   تھی

جمیلہ   پارک   میں   جھُولا   جھُول   رہی   تھی

جمیلہ   پارک   میں   جھُولا   جھُول   رہی   تھی

ملّا نے نواز بانسری بجا رہا تھا

ملّا نے نواز بانسری بجا رہا تھا

ملّا نے نواز بانسری بجا رہا تھا

ملّا نے نواز بانسری بجا رہا تھا

شامیانہ	

گُلدستہ	

بانسری	

سادھو کی دُعا

سادھو   درخت   کے   نیچے   عِبادت   کر رہا   تھا

سادھو   درخت   کے   نیچے   عِبادت   کر رہا   تھا

سادھو   درخت   کے   نیچے   عِبادت   کر رہا   تھا

سادھو   درخت   کے   نیچے   عِبادت   کر رہا   تھا

تھی کرتی چوں چوں چڑیا

تھی کرتی چوں چوں چڑیا

تھی کرتی چوں چوں چڑیا

تھی کرتی چوں چوں چڑیا

چِڑیا

لڑکی

لڑکے

گاؤں

سادُھو

بی گلہری

بادشاہ سلامت کی سواری آرہی ہے

بادشاہ سلامت کی سواری آرہی ہے

بادشاہ سلامت کی سواری آرہی ہے

بادشاہ سلامت کی سواری آرہی ہے

بی گلہری نے آم کا باغ خرید لیا

بی گلہری نے آم کا باغ خرید لیا

بی گلہری نے آم کا باغ خرید لیا

بی گلہری نے آم کا باغ خرید لیا

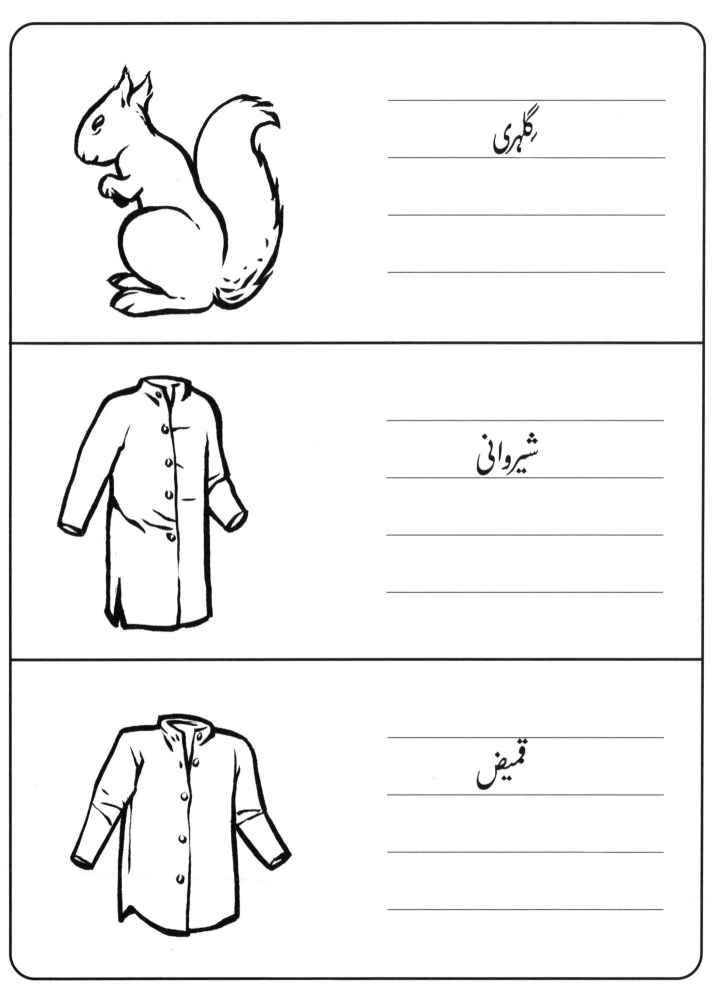

رگلہری

شیروانی

قمیض

ہاتھی

آم

بادشاہ

STRATEGIES FOR WRITING PRACTICE IN URDU AT HOME

- Encourage children to practise writing in *Let's Write Urdu*, one page at a time.

- If the children have difficulty writing, make a larger copy of the words from *Let's Write Urdu* and ask them to trace over them and then copy them.

- Give the students a few words at a time until they are comfortable with writing Urdu script.

- Regular practice (at least 15 minutes, three times a week) will help develop fluency in writing Urdu script.

Rashida Mirza

Note: In some Urdu words, the variation in spelling (as, for example, in the word and پیسا) has also been introduced.

WRITING PRACTICE

OBJECTIVES

To help the children enhance their writing skills.

To show the children the mechanics of writing in Urdu script.

To make the children aware of words and spaces.

STRATEGIES FOR THE INSTRUCTION OF WRITING IN URDU SCRIPT IN THE CLASSROOM

- in the beginning of the fall term, review the letters of the Urdu alphabet and have students practise joining letters to form words.

In subsequent sessions

- Have the children sit at the desks with pencils and exercise books.

- Choose five familiar words with the same initial letters or the same final letters from the current lesson.

- Demonstrate how each word is written, one word at a time, on the chalkboard or on the chart.

- Draw arrows to show the direction of each stroke.

- After writing each word, ask the students to copy it in their exercise books.

- When all five words have been copied, ask the children to write them three or four times.

The above practice will help the children to do the homework assigned using the *Let's Write Urdu* workbook.

stories and composed original music for the ten poems; he spent endless hours training a children's chorus for the musical versions of some poems, sang some poems solo, and also accompanied the children with sweet rhythms and melodies.

Anwer Saeed Ansari's help is gratefully acknowledged for providing handwritten Urdu sentences and vocabulary for writing-practice exercises for field-testing, and for his help in the preparation of camera-ready copy of *Let's Write Urdu* and *Let's Read Urdu*.

The long list of individuals who shaped and helped produce this work would not be complete without thanking the following: Saqib Mehmood, Institute of Islamic Culture, Lahore, for his assistance in getting the entire manuscript of the Urdu text computer-printed on short notice; Gavin McInnes for scanning the whole project (approximately 600 pages); Nargis Churchill for preparing disks of the camera-ready copy of all volumes except the *Teacher's Manual*; Robert Cameron for doing additional layout; Suroosh Alvi for giving advice on technical matters concerning printing and music recording, and for facilitating access to the artistic and technical talent available in Montreal; and Khadija Mirza for patiently typing several revisions of the *Teacher's Manual* and Introductory sections.

Special thanks as well to the McGill-Queen's University Press and its staff for their keen desire to publish this unusual work. Philip Cercone, executive director, appreciated the significance and intrinsic value of this project all along. This was particularly evident when the Press did not receive the expected publication subsidy from the Department of Multiculturalism in Ottawa and Philip was obliged to raise funds for this publication from various sources. Susanne McAdam, production and design manager, ably steered the course of production, and Joan McGilvray, coordinating editor, edited the English sections of the project and provided helpful suggestions on format and content.

The editor gratefully acknowledges permission to reprint the following copyrighted material: Orca Book Publisher, P.O. Box 5626, Postal Station B, Victoria, BC V8R 6S4, Canada, for "Maxine's Tree," and Shān al-Ḥaqq Ḥaqqī, for his published poem, "Bhā'ī Bhulakkar.

Sajida S. Alvi

Danesi's enthusiastic support of the project and his specific suggestions on methodology. He helped the team prepare the first lesson plan (for *Book One*) that was used as a model and has taken a keen interest in the project through the years.

Above all, I must acknowledge the unwavering commitment of the writing team members: Humaira Ansari, the late Firdaus Beg, Rashida Mirza, Zahida Murtaza, and Hamda Saifi. Their multiple roles did not deter them from putting in endless hours writing original stories and preparing creative lesson plans. The second phase was initiated in the beginning of 1993 while the work on the first phase was in its final stages. During the five-year period from 1993 to 1998, the entire group (the writing team, the project director, and the coordinators) spent long days together on weekends and holidays, evaluating and selecting the stories and revising, reviewing, and editing six or seven drafts of each story before field testing. Similarly, the lesson plans were also judiciously reviewed several times before their acceptance.

A special note in memory of Firdaus Beg, an imaginative, compassionate, and conscientious member of the team who fought cancer very courageously during the second phase of the project. In between her frequent visits to the hospital, she made sure to attend the meetings and put her heart and soul into the stories she wrote and the lesson plans she prepared while she was on sick leave from her school. Firdaus lost her valiant fight against cancer on March 17, 2002. The Project team dedicates this set of books to her. She is sorely missed.

Rupert Bottenberg, an artist in Montreal, showed the same commitment to the project as his counterparts in Toronto and Ottawa. Faruq Hassan's translations of the Urdu texts into English helped Rupert overcome the linguistic and cultural barriers, and he impressed the team with his creative and insightful interpretations of the stories through his art. Our special thanks to Rupert for the beautiful and detailed illustrations of the stories, poems, and flashcard vocabulary.

Farhat Ahmad, Faruq Hassan, and Ashfaq Hussain, the coordinators, were the anchors of our writing team. They ably supported the team in every aspect of the project. It was truly well-coordinated teamwork. In addition to my overall responsibility for the Project, Farhat Ahmad and I were intensely engaged in critiquing and editing the original Urdu stories by the team members and the lesson plans for the Teacher's Manual; Ashfaq Hussain and Faruq Hassan reviewed the stories, and typed them for field testing; Faruq Hassan compiled and typed the vocabulary lists; and Ashfaq Hussain spent endless hours in preparing camera-ready copy for McGill-Queen's University Press. Heart-felt thanks to them.

Our deep appreciation is due to those who worked equally hard to impart and preserve an important dimension of children's culture and heritage through sound and music. Jawaid Ahmad Danish and Uzma Danish brought the text of thirty stories to life through their audio recording in narrative style, providing auditory experience to complement the written text. And Nadeem Ali, an accomplished composer and singer, created background music for the

ACKNOWLEDGMENTS

Many institutions and individuals have worked on this project since its inception in 1990. Judy Young, the erstwhile director of the Heritage Languages Programme in the Department of Multiculturalism, ardently supported the project. The Canadian government's generous grant through her department resulted in the inception and completion of *Urdu for Children: Book One* and *Book Two*. Two other major partners in this venture are the former North York Board of Education (now part of the Toronto District School Board) and the Institute of Islamic Studies at McGill University. The North York Board and those involved in the International Languages Programme supported the project's housing, administration, and funding in addition to hosting regular meetings of the Project team members at the administration building. Among many individuals who worked at the North York Board of Education, special thanks go to Barbara Toye, Armando Cristinziano, and Susan Deschamps for their help and advice in the preparation of applications for funding to Ottawa, submission of progress reports, and careful preparation and implementation of the terms of various contracts signed by the Project team members.

The Institute of Islamic Studies has given substantive and material support to this project since my appointment to the endowed Chair in Urdu Language and Culture in 1986. This included secretarial help, bulk photocopying, postage, long-distance telephone calls, etc., as well as enthusiastic support for the book launch upon the completion of *Book One* in the fall of 1998. My frequent travel to Toronto for meetings with the Project team became part of my routine at the Institute. The publication of *Book Two* would not have been possible without the Institute's generous financial support. This timely assistance is gratefully acknowledged.

For the smooth field testing of the materials, our thanks are due to the following Boards of Education: in Metropolitan Toronto, York Region, North York, and Peel Boards, and in Ottawa, the Carleton Board. Special thanks go to these members of the Steering Committee: Irene Blayney (Carleton Board), Dr. Marcel Danesi (University of Toronto), Armando Cristinziano and Barbara Toye (North York Board), Izhar Mirza (National Federation of Pakistani Canadians), and Joseph Pizzolante (Etobicoke Board).

On substantive matters, Marcel Danesi, professor of Italian studies, University of Toronto, and James Cummins, professor of education at the Ontario Institute for Studies in Education, made invaluable contributions. The team is especially appreciative of Professor

growth in the South Asian community in Canada, a majority of whom have come from the Indo-Pakistan subcontinent where Urdu/Hindi is used as a lingua franca. In the 1986 census, the number of Canadians of South Asian origin was 266,800;* by 1991, it was 420,295, an increase of 57.5 per cent. In the 1996 census, the number jumped to 670,585, an increase of 59.5 per cent; and in the 2001 census the number has jumped to 963,190, an increase of 43.6 per cent. We hope that *Urdu for Children: Book One* and *Book Two* will help meet the needs of a rapidly increasing younger generation of the Urdu/Hindi-speaking community in Canada, the United States, and Europe.

The Urdu Language Textbook Series is the first step towards helping children develop Urdu linguistic skills so that they can keep the flame of their heritage and culture alive. In today's global village, knowledge of a third language, and particularly a non-European language such as Urdu, can certainly help Canadian children become proud and self-assured adults and a unique asset to Canadian society. Indeed, cultural and linguistic diversity can be a major source of enrichment in any social and political order. Thomas Homer-Dixon's warning that, in the current race for globalisation, languages and cultures are disappearing at an alarming rate is noteworthy. Such languages, he argues, should be protected and preserved because we need cultural and linguistic diversity to help solve our problems and resolve our conflicts, in the same way that we need varied ecosystems.**

Sajida S. Alvi

---

* Pamela M. White & Atul Nanda, "South Asians in Canada," *Canadian Social Trends* (Autumn, 1989): 7–9.

** Thomas Homer-Dixon, "We Need a Forest of Tongues." The *Globe and Mail*, July 7, 2001.

settes, a workbook, and a teacher's manual. This work was the first of its kind in terms of the quality of its content, its sensitivity to the needs of children between the ages of four to six in the Canadian environment, and its eclectic combination of traditional and whole-language instructional methods.

This publication was seen as a fitting testament to the commitment of the Department of Multiculturalism to producing quality instructional materials for Canadian children through the International Languages Programme. This programme demonstrates that, while the English and French languages represent the linguistic duality of this nation, there is a place for other international languages, including Urdu, in the rich Canadian mosaic. For the Project team, it was also a way of joining in the celebration of the Golden Jubilee of the birth of Pakistan, where Urdu is the official language of a nation of over 140 million people.

The current book in the series, *Urdu for Children: Stories and Poems*, while similar to the first in methodology, is designed to meet the needs of children between the ages of seven to eight and older. The students' level is based on their facility in reading, writing, and speaking the language rather than their chronological age. The scope of the topics is wider than in Book One, and the forty stories and poems (most of them original and some adapted) are more complex and longer, and the original artwork is richer and more varied. More details are given in the section "About This Book." The English-Urdu and Urdu-English vocabulary lists are more comprehensive than for Book One. Two volumes of *Let's Read Urdu* have been added to help children enhance their reading skills. The two-part *Let's Write Urdu* workbook provides practice exercises in writing and reinforces the new vocabulary introduced in the texts. The *Teacher's Manual* is a comprehensive, activities-based guide for teachers and parents and provides detailed lesson plans for each Urdu text. Two carefully recorded CDs accompanying the two volumes of the textbook, ensure standard pronunciation of words and intonations in sentences, and infuse life into the stories. Original music was composed for the poems, with melodies created for children to sing to help memorize the poems. From the inception of this project, we have kept in mind the needs of children as well as the needs of those parents who have some familiarity with the Urdu language and who wish to be involved in helping their children learn the Urdu language.

The *Urdu for Children* Textbook Series was envisioned as a model that could be adapted for other non-European heritage languages, especially for South Asian languages such as Hindi, Bengali, Punjabi and languages of predominantly Muslim regions such as Arabic, Dari, Persian, Pashto and Sindhi. The Project team sincerely hopes that this vision will be realized in the coming years by the next generation of teachers and policy-makers. It would be a small but significant step in furthering the spirit of multiculturalism by promoting pride in the many Canadian cultural identities. The development of proper instructional materials for the Urdu language shows the commitment of Canadians of Indo-Pakistani origin to safeguarding their rich cultural heritage for future generations. There has been a rapid

THE STORY BEHIND THIS PROJECT

The remarkable story of the Urdu Instructional Materials Development Project began in 1986 when I returned to McGill University as the first appointee to the Chair in Urdu Language and Culture after an absence of nine years from the Canadian scene. During the time I had taught at the University of Minnesota (1977–86), the concept of multiculturalism was developing roots and taking concrete shape through Canadian government policies. The government's Heritage Languages Program, under the auspices of the Department of Multiculturalism, began sponsoring the development of instructional materials in a variety of heritage languages. On my return to Canada, Izhar Mirza, then president of the National Federation of Pakistani Canadians, and the late Muinudin Muin, both community leaders and friends, drew my attention to the need to develop proper Urdu language instructional tools for children. Consequently in May 1990, with funding from the Department of Multiculturalism, we held a one-day conference at McGill University, jointly sponsored by the Federation of Pakistani Canadians and the Institute of Islamic Studies. Its purpose was to assess the need to develop instructional materials in Urdu and to look for people to work on this project. A team of writers and coordinators was established. Thus began the arduous work of a group of individuals, divergent in their backgrounds and professional training but united by a deep sense of mission. Undeterred by difficulties of commuting from Montreal and Ottawa, and within Metropolitan Toronto, the Project team worked for long hours on the weekends and holidays for over seven years to produce two sets of books. In the initial stages of the project, I realized that the members of the writing team who joined the enterprise had the invaluable experience of classroom teaching in the public school system but no experience of writing and publishing. This did not discourage us, however. Through their sheer determination, motivation, and willingness to write several drafts of each story until everyone was satisfied, the team of full-time teachers in the Ontario Boards of Education was transformed into a team of proficient creative storywriters and authors. This was a very gratifying experience for me.

In August 1997, the Urdu Instructional Materials Development Project team members and various Boards of Education in Ontario involved in the project celebrated the Silver Jubilee of the multicultural policy of the Government of Canada with the publication of *Urdu for Children: Book One*. This groundbreaking work, which provides instruction in Urdu for children, is comprised of two volumes of texts accompanied by two audiocas-

CONTENTS

English Section

The Story Behind This Project
Acknowledgments
Writing Practice

Urdu Section